VOCAL / PIANO

CONTENTS

2   ALWAYS ON MY MIND

8   AVE MARIA

14   CUORE

20   FALLING

25   LONGER

30   MY WAY

40   NEED YOU NOW

46   ON A NIGHT LIKE THIS

51   ROADS

58   UNLESS YOU MEAN IT

64   VIVA LA VIDA

Photography by Randee St. Nicholas

ISBN 978-1-4803-4079-4

7777 W. BLUEMOUND RD. P.O. BOX 13819 MILWAUKEE, WI 53213

Visit Hal Leonard Online at
www.halleonard.com

ALWAYS ON MY MIND

Words and Music by WAYNE THOMPSON,
MARK JAMES and JOHNNY CHRISTOPHER

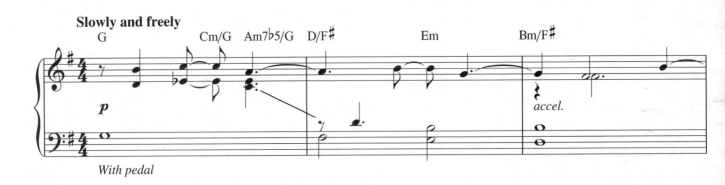

AVE MARIA

By FRANZ SCHUBERT
Arranged by WALTER AFANASIEFF

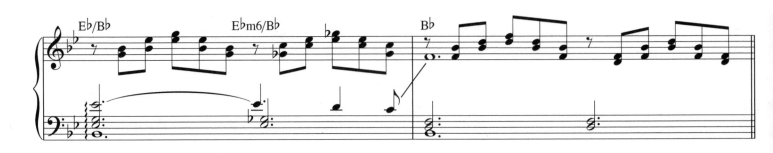

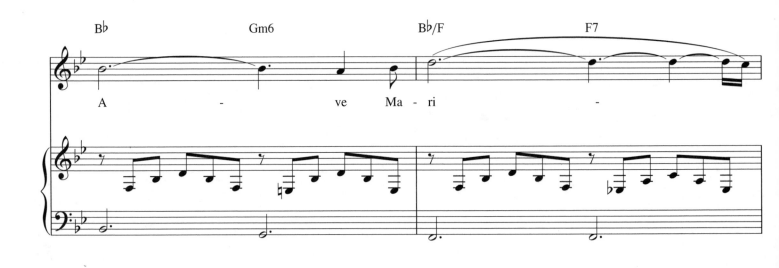

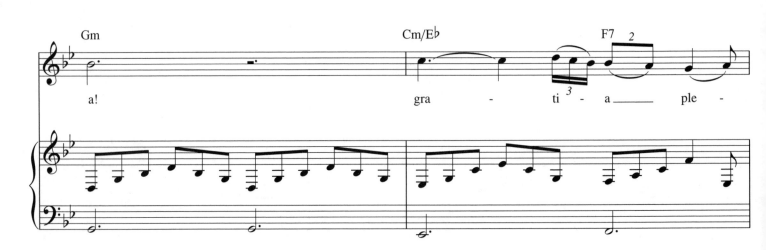

10

CUORE

Words and Music by CHRIS MANN,
MARCO MARINANGELI and SAVAN KOTECHA

FALLING

Words and Music by CHRIS MANN,
KEITH THOMAS and LIZ ROSE

LONGER

Words and Music by
DAN FOGELBERG

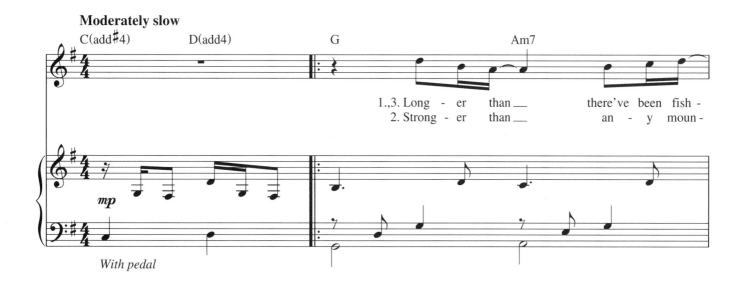

1.,3. Long - er than __ there've been fish -
2. Strong - er than __ an - y moun -

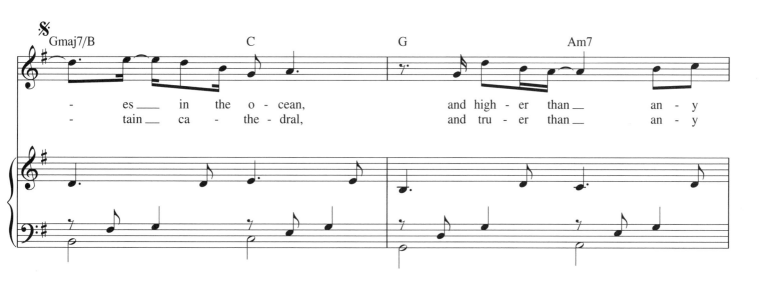

- es __ in the o - cean, and high - er than __ an - y
- tain __ ca - the - dral, and tru - er than __ an - y

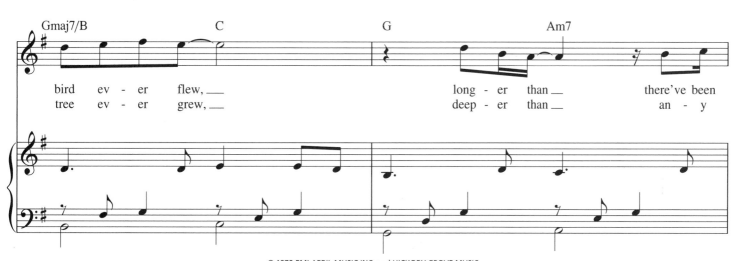

bird ev - er flew, __ long - er than __ there've been
tree ev - er grew, __ deep - er than __ an - y

MY WAY

English Words by PAUL ANKA
Original French Words by GILLES THIBAULT
Music by JACQUES REVAUX and CLAUDE FRANCOIS

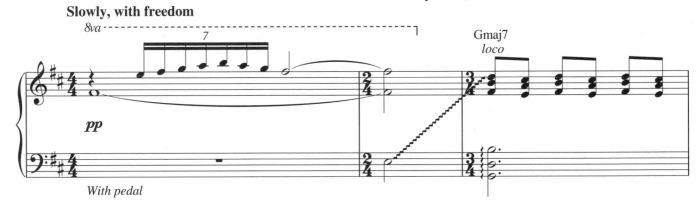

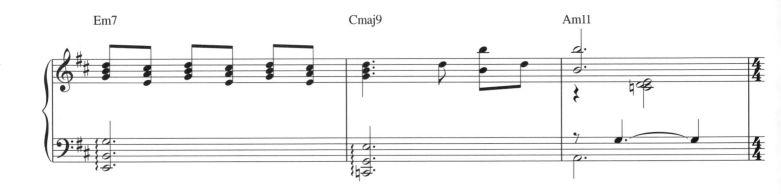

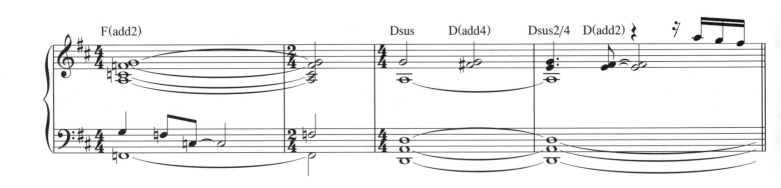

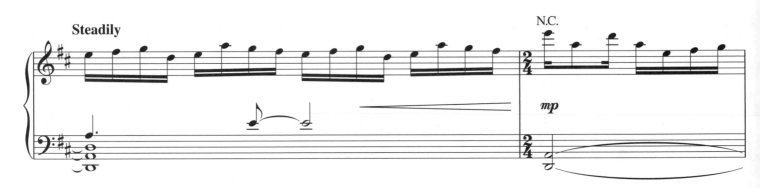

NEED YOU NOW

Words and Music by HILLARY SCOTT,
CHARLES KELLEY, DAVE HAYWOOD
and JOSH KEAR

Moderately slow half-time feel

With pedal

Pic - ture per - fect mem - 'ries
oth - er shot of whis - key;

scat - tered all a - round the floor; ___
can't stop look - ing at the door. ___

ON A NIGHT LIKE THIS

Words and Music by
DAVE BARNES

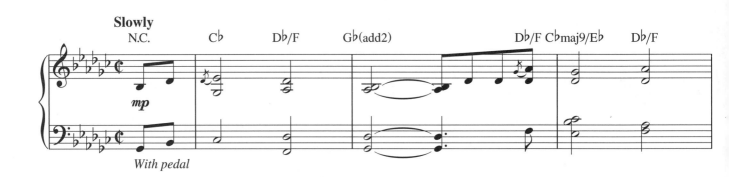

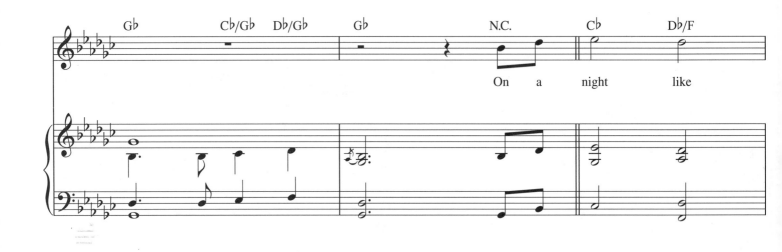

On a night like

this, I could fall in love; I could

ROADS

Words and Music by DIDRIK THOTT,
CARL FREDRIK BJORSELL, TEBEY OTTOH
and SEBASTIAN THOTT

There ___ are ___ roads in this life that we ___ all trav- el; there are

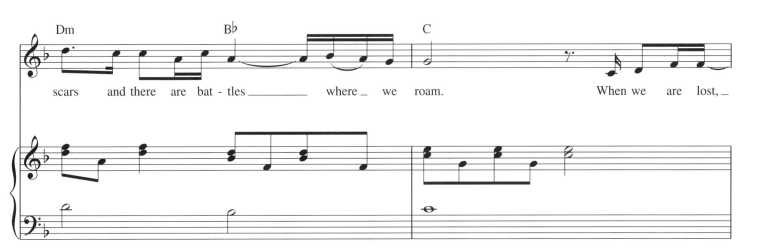

scars and there are bat- tles ___ where ___ we roam. When we are lost, ___

___ or wher- ev- er we ___ may go, ___ they will

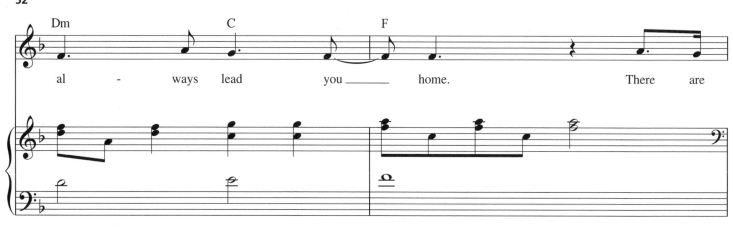

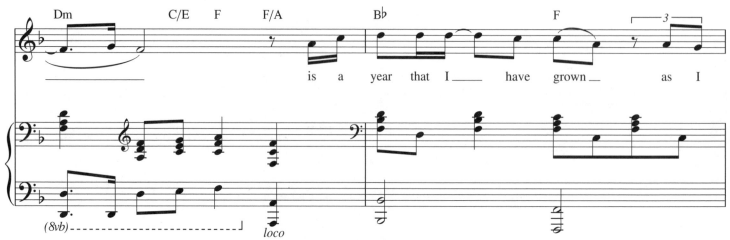

UNLESS YOU MEAN IT

Words and Music by
WILLIAM JAMES McAULEY

VIVA LA VIDA

Words and Music by GUY BERRYMAN,
JON BUCKLAND, WILL CHAMPION
and CHRIS MARTIN